The Doctrine of Exquisite
PRECIOUSNESS

The Doctrine of Exquisite
PRECIOUSNESS

JOE HARDY

The Doctrine of Exquisite Preciousness
by Joe C. Hardy
© 2025 by Ellerslie Press

ISBN 978-1-943592-87-6

Ellerslie Press
Windsor, CO

Published in the United States of America.

To my father who modeled it,
to my wife who inspired it,
and to the Ludy Boys who helped write it.
Soli Deo Gloria!

Contents

Joe Hardy Action Mode

When my 83-year-old aunt heard that I was writing a book, she slammed her coffee mug down on the table and exclaimed to my mother, "Margie, you must stop him! That book will only be an embarrassment to the good Hardy name."

My elderly mother, Margaret, sitting across the table from her, sighed and said, "I know Carol, but when Joe makes up his mind to do something — you know how he gets."

Since you haven't spent fifty-four years learning the ins and outs of Joseph Carroll Hardy Sr., it's possible that when my mother declares, "You know how he gets," that you actually don't know how I get. So I'll tell you.

I get a wry smile on my face, a chuckle in my throat, a glint in my eye, and my right hand balls up into a fist.

Sounds harmless, doesn't it? But, according to my dear mother and my Aunt Carol, this so-called Joe Hardy

Action Mode was precisely what led to my broken leg and head contusion in Moab, my three-week hospitalization in Malawi, my tiger bite in Bhutan resulting in the loss of two beloved toes, and the permanent scar running down my back that I picked up going over that waterfall in Brazil in that flimsy canoe.

Okay. I'll admit it. There are some dire consequences to my having a hankering for impossible adventures. But what my Aunt Carol and dear mother fail to bring up are the countless treasures that I've obtained because of that very same "Joe Hardy Action Mode."

There was the Golden Urn of Shapito that I unearthed in the salt mines of Vietnam just minutes before it was flooded by the tsunami in '78; the Mayan treasure wrested from the grubby hands of thieves in El Salvador in '75; and how about the ten thousand doubloons discovered in that underwater Peruvian cave in '74?

But beyond mere earthly treasure, there's the relational treasure gained in and through my — ahem — propensity for doing dangerous things. For instance, there was the peace treaty I negotiated between the Sewti natives and the Shimmi refugees in the jungle valley of the Morro Do Fogão, as well as the sparing of an entire village from a volcanic eruption in '76 because I dared to jump inside it and find out if it was still active.

My mother is correct. Regarding the writing of this book, I have indeed gone into "Joe Hardy Action Mode." And though I realize that this book could very well embarrass the good Hardy name, I believe that it is more than worth the risk.

I told Bruce and Steve, the producers of my television show, this morning that I'm retiring from the show after we wrap the next episode in Burma. *Salt Worthy Adventures* has had a great ten-year run. But I have something bigger than television that I feel I need to do with my life. It's an idea that my Aunt Carol considers to be "dumber than a dung beetle's diet," and my dear mother figures it to be "evidence I'm experiencing a delayed mid-life crisis."

I realize I've never written a book. And since I've been in television since I was twenty-two, I guess I can understand their pause and concern with me retiring from it.

But I've made up my mind. And I'm convinced that it will be a repeat of the Amazon Miracle of '79.

In 1979, I announced I was going to produce a three episode mini-series of *Salt Worthy Adventures* tracing Theodore Roosevelt's historic and perilous journey through the Amazon Jungle. Per usual, Aunt Carol flew off the handle and warned that I would get malaria if I did. And guess what? I got malaria — *bad*. But I also found a priceless treasure in the midst of that adventure. I found a little baby girl on the embankment of the Rio da Dúvida. She had been abandoned and sacrificed to the wild.

When I picked her tiny little starving body up in my arms, I knew in that moment the six weeks of malaria and dysentery were totally worth it. That little girl, Preciosa, is still alive today because I went into Joe Hardy Action Mode.

Even if this book never sells one copy, I think it is still worth writing. Because it's my way of putting to paper my vision. *This* is what I want to do with the rest of my life. I think it's important, even if I'm spelling it out only for myself.

But I do hope that somehow the book sells at least one copy and gets into your hands. And that as you read its contents, my vision may become your vision as well. For when we risk the malaria, the dysentery, and the harsh words of Aunt Carol, we position ourselves to find a baby Preciosa on the embankment.

What would I be willing to do to rescue another Preciosa? That question has been ringing in my soul now for the past five years. And I've finally arrived at my answer.

For a start, I'm quitting my television show and I'm writing this book.

But that is only the beginning.

I call it the Doctrine of Exquisite Preciousness.

Beware. It's catching. And I hope one day soon you too will get a wry smile on your face, a chuckle in your throat, a glint in your eye, and your right hand will ball up into a fist.

Chapter One

The Billiard Ball

My mother and Aunt Carol have always struggled with my danger-filled life choices.

I can blame my late father for that because, basically, I'm him with hair.

My dad's name was Billy. At least that is what my mother called him. Technically, the name on his birth certificate was William. But not a soul on earth ever called him William. The Billiard Ball was his famous nickname, which his friends shortened to B. B.

Billy "B. B." Hardy — rabid adventurer, newspaper journalist, and radio personality. He was bald as the rump of a baboon with the raucous laugh of a bonobo. He could make friends with an angry rhino or cuddle up with a sleeping grizzly bear and get a wonderful night's sleep. He was just that way. If it was a crazy idea, he was into it.

My dad snacked on danger for breakfast, and my mother lived in a constant state of anxiety because of it.

My Aunt Carol prognosticated my father's untimely death in 1948, saying, "Margie, if Billy keeps going on these harebrained adventures — like heading out to photograph polar bears — one day he's going to get himself killed." She, unfortunately, proved to be correct. My father died three weeks later when I was eighteen. We still don't know exactly what happened or even what the precise cause of his death was, but we do know he was in the Arctic on a grand adventure when he passed. Jacques Salon, his ever-faithful photographer traveling with him, apparently witnessed the whole thing and somehow crawled back to their basecamp, writing down in his journal the words *Polar bears were…BB would not…* before he himself died from loss of blood.

As a result of this rather traumatizing event, I've actually been resistant toward any trips to the Arctic region and have strategically avoided being around polar bears my entire adult life.

But the reason I bring up my father is not just because he's to blame for my danger-filled lifestyle, but because he is also the primary reason for this book.

He personally taught me the Doctrine of Exquisite Preciousness.

Of course, he didn't call it that, but it's the essence of how he lived out his life.

My father believed that God, as Creator, made this great big world to reveal His awesome nature. And he believed that by exploring its wilds, scaling its dangers, and crossing its rapids, he would better discover and get to know this God of the Wild.

"Joey," he said to me when I was twelve, standing next to him atop Mount Kilimanjaro, "I brought you here to introduce you to God."

The view from that high peak was staggering, enormous, grand, and awe-inspiring. In that rarified moment, he showed me that those were the same qualities my God possessed.

I remember him meeting my gaze and saying, "The God that created all *this* is the same God that gave up everything to save *you*!"

I grew up attending a small Baptist church in New Braunfels, Texas, so I had heard all about Jesus, the Cross, the empty tomb, and all the wonders that followed. But, *that* moment, standing on the peak of Kilimanjaro next to my father, was when I owned it.

I saw how big God was and, at the same time, how profound, ridiculous, and mind-blowing it was that such a big God took interest in such a tiny little critter like me.

My father was an exceptional man. And though I only enjoyed eighteen years with him, he made an indelible imprint upon my life.

Chapter Two

The Legend of B. B. Hardy

To lay the foundation in your understanding of the Doctrine of Exquisite Preciousness, I would like to use my father as a muse.

He lived out this doctrine before my eyes.

Let me give you seven profound ways in which he demonstrated it to me.

Number One: My father gave away fifty percent of his income.

When my mother questioned his philosophy of benevolence, I remember him simply saying, "God gives us Hardys more than we require so that we can bless those that have less than they need."

Number Two: My father tipped one hundred percent at restaurants.

I would have never known this except for a time the two of us ate at a little hole-in-the-wall cafe in Tennessee when we were traveling together in 1947. The manager came running out of the restaurant yelling after my father, "Sir! Sir! You left money on the table."

"Oh, did I?" replied my dad.

The man held out the cash for my dad to take.

My dad simply said, "What makes you think I want it back?"

The man replied, "I told Beatrice that it must have been an accident. No one tips one hundred percent."

My dad smiled and said, "You go tell Beatrice that there is someone on this earth that does in fact tip one hundred percent, and that I hope she's as blessed in receiving it as I was in receiving her excellent service."

Number Three: My father was a father to the fatherless.

In our small community of New Braunfels, my father helped start up a program he called BBC. It was an acronym for "Baptist Boys Club." At any given time from 1938 to when he died in 1948, he always had at least one boy in the community that he was personally investing into, taking camping, teaching how to swing a baseball bat, inviting over for dinner, or helping with their science homework.

In 1945, a woman named Barbara Tomkins wrote a letter to my father asking if he could make an exception to his "boys only" rule and possibly lend a hand to a fourteen-year-old girl named Lucille who had recently lost her father in the war and her mother to cancer. My father agreed.

Lucy turned out to be quite an amazing young woman. She was adopted by an older couple in our church, graduated at the top of her class a few years later, and went on to get a doctoral degree in archeology from Yale.

Oh, and did I mention that in 1955, I was so impressed with this girl named Lucy that I asked her to marry me? And just in case you're wondering. She said yes.

Number Four: My father had a huge heart for the small and forgotten.

Bert Calloway was an elderly crippled man who lived in a shanty on the east side of town. He had no family and no friends. To my father, Bert was the most important man in the world.

Every Sunday, my father drove ten minutes out of the way to pick him up for church. Then Bert would always enjoy Sunday dinner at the Hardy house and even take an afternoon nap on our couch.

Bert died in 1945. He had written up a last will and testament that he left lying on his kitchen counter. It read:

> *Everything I have goes to my best friend, B. B. Hardy. He gave everything to me in my time of need. I don't have any family, so I'm bequeathing every thing I own to him. I don't actually have anything to give, but he can have the shark tooth.*

It was my father who had given Bert that shark tooth for his eighty-sixth birthday two years prior. My dad cherished that final gift from his dear friend Bert, wearing the tooth around his neck proudly until the end.

Number Five: My father considered the small people the biggest people.

My father taught me that Beatrice the waitress at Conner's Cafe in Nashville, Tennessee (and every single person like her) was valuable. And it wasn't just through his exorbitant tipping standards — it went beyond that. He would always leave little notes on the table for the kitchen help before he got up to leave a restaurant. His notes usually read something like, "You guys do great work. Thanks for serving us today. May God bless you!"

My father genuinely cared about the small people that served.

Number Six: My father saw extreme value in the underprivileged and thought they deserved the very best.

He taught me that little kids missing a father or a mother were the apple of God's eye. He treated them like royalty. He would pay for their dental work, their eye exams and glasses, their new shoes, and shiny new bicycles. His reasoning was: if these little ones didn't have a father to do these things for them, then he'd better step in and do it. Because isn't that precisely what his Father in Heaven did for him at the Cross?

Very few people ever get to see this sort of behavior up close. I think that's why people don't quite know how to respond to the Heavenly Father when they are introduced to His exorbitant love and generosity.

Maybe it's just too extravagant for their human understanding.

My father was merely a modest introduction to a much more fabulous Father.

Number Seven: My father taught me about mercy and second chances.

Before Jacques Salon became my father's faithful photographer and traveled the world with him, he spent ten years in prison for money laundering. Jacques had once been a world famous talent. Now he was tainted goods. But not to my father. To my father, he was exactly the sort of man fit for the job of being his close friend and companion on dangerous adventures.

As previously mentioned, before Jacques Salon died in 1948, he wrote down in his journal the words *Polar bears were... BB would not*. Over the past thirty-six years, I've pondered those words a thousand and one times. And I think I've come to a pretty solid conclusion as to what Jacques was attempting to express.

I think he was trying to say, "Polar bears were coming after me, but BB would not let them have me."

Of course, I can't prove that. But I certainly saw my dad live it — the Doctrine of Exquisite Preciousness in living color.

B. B. Hardy. That's the kind of man I want to grow up to be like.

Chapter Three

Lucy Packs Her Suitcase

So what exactly is the Doctrine of Exquisite Preciousness?

I've struggled to know how to put into words something that took me fifty- plus years to finally figure out.

If I were to give a dictionary definition for it, it might be "the shockingly merciful attitude of God toward me, toward you, and toward every other human being on earth."

But I'm not sure that is enough to explain it.

Here's another dictionary-styled definition for you to chew on:

> It's the way God thinks toward the unlovely, the smelly, the backwards, and the bucktoothed. And it's the way that He invites me to think towards them as well.

Those definitions are both true, and maybe they work for you. But I'm a three-dimensional kind of guy. I learn by climbing a truth, crossing the cold waters of an idea in my soul's bare feet, and seeing the concept with the eyes of my inner man.

To me, the Doctrine of Exquisite Preciousness is shaped like a person. And that person, in my imagination, is about five-foot-three with long blonde hair and a cute button nose. She's feisty as a mountain cougar and sports the name Lucy Hardy.

I was married to Lucy Hardy for twenty-seven years before she was taken from me by that same doggone cancer that took her mother from her.

When I think of the Doctrine of Exquisite Preciousness, I can't help but think of Lucy.

Like Lucy, this idea is strikingly beautiful but tough as nails. It's gentle as a fragrant breeze but backed by a thunderclap.

"Joey," Lucy would always say to me with hands on hips, "you need to go back and make that right."

"What?" I would always say, feigning innocence. "What did I do this time?"

"You did nothing right, that's what you did," she would say kindly but firmly. And she would not back down. I outsized her by a foot and outweighed her by over a hundred pounds, but she won every verbal arm wrestle we ever enjoyed.

I hadn't behave like Jesus and she wouldn't relent until I woke up to that fact and made it right with the poor person I'd unwittingly harmed. And she made sure I always did.

"You just walked right past that sweet girl!" she said to me when we were in New York City in '63. "Didn't you see that cute thing?"

"No," I said brusquely, "should I have?"

"Yes, as a matter of fact," she huffed, "you should have!"

"And may I ask," I replied, still attempting to walk towards Central Park, "why exactly does it matter?"

"Because, you big pottamus," she said with her tough-as-nails-thunder-clap side on full display, "she had her hand stretched out toward you. She was asking you to assist her."

"You've got to be kidding me!" I shot back. "You just described a third of New York City. Luce — it's all a ruse. Those sort are doing their begging to fleece the naive."

I remember Lucy's response as if it were yesterday.

"Joseph Carroll Hardy!" she stated firmly with a staccato ring to her voice, "Your dad taught you better than that, didn't he? What would he have done? Would he just shrug and walk on by?"

"Let me repeat," I countered, "it's a ruse!"

"So what if it is?" she said. "What if it is a ruse? Your job isn't to police everyone's motives, Joe. It's to behave like a citizen of Heaven."

As I try and put shape and dimension to this idea of the Doctrine of Exquisite Preciousness, that right there is it for me.

I am programmed as a human toward equity, justice, and fairness. Those are my top priorities. And I can walk right by that sweet girl in New York City because I've judged her to be fraudulent. But God's top priorities are love, mercy, and outrageous generosity. So, although that girl *could* be running a scam, God first sees the value of that girl and not the girl's sin. He first sees the potential of that girl and not just the girl's present misbehavior.

God stops for the girl. He actually stops. He bends down. He smiles. He inconveniences Himself with her life. Why? Because to Him, this girl is exquisitely precious. He loves her.

The question is: will Joe Hardy stop, stoop, listen, and love her too?

For you, the Doctrine of Exquisite Preciousness may not be five-foot-three Lucy Hardy. It may be four-foot-one or seven-foot-two, but it's carrying the same heavenly dynamic in its tote bag.

I just happen to picture the Holy Spirit of God looking a lot like my beloved wife and acting a lot like her too. I picture Lucy packing up her suitcase, sticking on those red leather high heels, and coming to live inside my heart. She grabs my eyes and turns them to see what God sees. She touches my mind to think what God thinks. She moves my heart to feel what God feels. And she guides my hands and feet to match precisely what God's hands and feet would be doing in response.

Oh, I know that the Holy Spirit and my dear wife are not the same. But sometimes you just need to get a mental picture in your mind to grasp the mysterious ways that God works.

Joe, I hear this Inner Lucy say to me all throughout the day, *Jesus loves them. Will you?*

Chapter Four

Steer to the Shore

Choosing to quit my television show will probably sound like a brash, rash decision to those who don't know what's been swirling around inside my heart and mind over these past few years.

I can trace it back to February 2, 1979. As previously mentioned, I had spent the previous six weeks attempting to survive a rather extreme bout with malaria. I had lain on a flimsy cot in a small medical facility near Araras for what had seemed like forever.

As I lay there in misery, I thought about my life. I was about to turn fifty. I thought of Lucy, and how unfair it was that I had chosen this adventure over her. I thought of our only child, Joseph Jr. — eleven at the time — and how pitiful my investment had been into his life thus far. I had chosen danger and daring over faithfulness and fathering.

As I lay there, wondering if this day, February 2, would be my last day, I sensed God speak to me.

You have lived fifty years for Joe. Now will you live the rest of your life for Me? If so, you will be healed.

It wasn't audible. No one around me seemed to hear it. But it was a question that had teeth, and it bit into my heart.

I whispered out loud, "Yes, Lord! I will!"

That day I recovered from both my bout with malaria and my terrible dysentery. That day I experienced a miracle. That day marked a new beginning in my life. I had the number one show on television. I had fame. I had influence. But all of those things suddenly felt like worthless pablum.

There was something more to life. I had just brushed up against it. I wanted to get home to Lucy and just hold her and tell her how much I loved her. I wanted to lift Joseph Jr. up into my arms and kiss every square inch of his face. I wanted to live a life that would show God how truly grateful I was for His mercy and kindness.

It wasn't but three days later that I saw Preciosa on the shoreline of the great river, abandoned, lying in her waste. I remember yelling to the boatmaster, "Stop! Steer to the shore!"

The boatmaster, when he saw why we were headed toward the shore, shouted, "Leave it, Señor Hardy. It's not for you — it's for the *Yacuruna*."

I simply said, "Steer to the shore, Carlos."

When I picked her up and held her in my arms, something broke inside me. This little life didn't belong to a false river god; it belonged to the true Almighty God.

Staring down at her precious face, I realized — maybe for the first time — what life was really all about.

God was speaking to me. And if I could put the heavenly impression into a paragraph it would sound like this:

Joe, you were my fragile little helpless Preciosa, about to be ravaged by the Amazon wilds. But I saw you there, lying in your filth, and I came to this earth — just for you — to rescue you. Remember, Joe — what I have done unto you — you must now do unto the many other Preciosas lying on the shoreline of life needing someone, anyone, to care and share the love of Jesus with them.

A high percentage of the world would not consider Preciosa worth much. But, on February 2, five years ago, I discovered that the exact opposite was true.

Preciosa is exquisitely precious.

Chapter Five

A Square Foot
of Dirt

I'm writing this in September of 1984. My beloved Lucy passed away two years ago July. Joey, my son, is now sixteen. And though it pains me to realize I lost nearly fifty years in selfish living, I'm forever grateful for the change of heart and life that God brought to me in February of 1979.

Not a day has gone by since that I don't reflect upon what it means to "quit living for Joe and start living for Jesus."

This past March, I was doing some research on international real estate investing. When looking at the value of Mediterranean shoreline property, I was shocked at the price tag. So, out of pure intrigue, I ventured into a tangential study on the most expensive real estate property in the world.

Here's what I found. The most expensive real estate property per square foot in the world is found in Monaco.

Get this. It costs a staggering $60,000 for a square foot of dirt in Monaco. Sixty grand — for twelve square inches!

This got me thinking.

What causes Monaco dirt to be worth so much?

Simply put: the reason Monaco real estate is valued so high is because someone is willing to pay that much for it.

The price is directly related to the demand.

Someone, somewhere has determined that they really love Monaco property, and they are willing to give up *a lot* in order to purchase it.

And this is when it hit me.

Monaco dirt is not the most expensive real estate in the world. Nope. Not by a long shot. The most expensive real estate in the world is the Human Life — body, soul, and spirit.

God paid for it with His very *Life*.

How does Acts 20:28 say it: "Jesus purchased us with His own blood"?

How much is Jesus's blood worth?

According to the Bible, it's "precious, priceless" — it's of inestimable value.

So, if the shed blood of Jesus is priceless and He purchased us with this priceless blood, what does that make us worth?

This is the Doctrine of Exquisite Preciousness.

Forget Monaco. According to God, the human life is the most valuable real estate in the world.

That means that a square inch of Preciosa, Beatrice, or Bert Calloway is worth exceedingly more than the entire 12,566 feet of coastline of Monaco.

Chapter Six

Joey Day

Being a single father with a sixteen-year-old boy in the home could certainly be cause for some concern.

I admit, I don't have Lucy's touch at home — with cooking, with nursing, with discipline, or with those parental heart-to-heart bedside chats.

But where there is lack in Joe Hardy, I sense that God has given me wisdom for the task and is helping to make up the difference. In fact, I actually think Joey Jr. is going to turn out alright — somehow surviving losing his mother at fourteen and getting stuck with me as his dad.

That said, I must admit, there have been some rough patches along the way.

I came home from my great Amazon adventure in '79 and for a few weeks, I really was great at home. I started speaking into Joey's life. I would write him a daily note of encouragement. I would pray for him every time he came into my mind. I would give him a hug and a kiss on the forehead every time I left or arrived home. I even started coming to his bedside at night as he was preparing to sleep and try and do one of those heart-to-heart chats.

But after the twenty-third day of "Amazing Joe," I regressed back to my "Old Joe" ways with my son.

Don't get me wrong. The change from February 2 was real. I had begun to finally see the Preciosas around me. I would carry a hundred dollars in cash in my pocket everywhere I went and ask God to show me who needed it most that day. I was praying for those in my life who were sick, those who were lost, and those who needed practical encouragement. I was really changed. But I wasn't really changed in my fatherhood.

It was strange. I had boundless mercy for the filthy, immoral people on the streets of Los Angeles (where we were living at the time), but I would get frustrated with Joey for giving me a disrespectful sideways glance.

I could endure spit and spiteful words from the homeless on Alameda Street, but if Joey forgot to wash off his dish after dinner, I would explode with a diatribe of how disrespectful he was being to his father.

Tuesday, June 21, 1983 was another big day in my life. I refer to it affectionately as Joey Day.

I was filming a special edition of *Salt Worthy Adventures* in Ireland. Joey had traveled with me on this trip and the two of us were scaling the Cliffs of Moher in County Clare. We had just gotten started on our journey up the cliff face when Joey's rope snapped. He fell at least thirty feet onto the rocks below.

I thought he was dead. As I stared down the rocky wall and saw his body laying there totally still, I remembered the preciousness of my son.

As I stared, I also remembered that moment on February 2 in 1979 in Brazil while I lay there dying with malaria. I remembered God healing me. So I thought, *God can heal Joey!*

Clinging helplessly to the cliffside, I cried out to God. "Lord, take me instead. Please. Let Joey live. Please."

As I finished my tearful pleading, suddenly I saw Joey move. Then Joey sat up. Then he looked up. Then he smiled. Then he gave me a thumbs up.

I made a vow to God in that moment: "Joey gets my best, Lord. Not my leftovers. My son gets my best."

Joey Day solidified something inside me. I resolved at that very second: "I'm going to retire from this show as soon as my contract expires, and I'm going to prioritize being a father to this precious boy in my life. He's going to get the best of my energies, the best of my love, and the best of my time."

Chapter Seven

Dinner at the Ivy

This past March 2, I wrote a letter to Joey.

I taped it to his bathroom mirror so that when he woke up that morning, he wouldn't miss it.

I had just finished my research on the value of real estate in Monaco and finally had words to express what had been stirring inside me. I wanted to bring Joey in on my discovery.

Here's what I wrote:

March 2nd, 1984

Son,

You are aware that I've been looking for a property for us to purchase. But in my search, I found something I wasn't expecting to find. I just stumbled across the most valuable real estate in the world. I think you might find it fabulously flabbergasting.

Because the most valuable real estate in the world is YOU!

Worth the shed blood of Jesus Christ,

Worth His Almighty Life given up,
Worth God coming to Earth to save,
Worth God Himself suffering and dying,
Of inestimable, unfathomable worth.
In light of this exciting discovery, I would like
to run an idea by you, Joey.
How about dinner tonight? You game?
Dad

Joey and I met for dinner that night at The Ivy. I had an idea burning a hot hole inside my heart, and I needed to share it with him.

We had just finished our dinner when I divulged the idea.

"Joey," I said, "I'm sorry if I came across as distracted this past week."

"No worries," he said with a smirk, "I survived the parental negligence."

"Well, I just want you to know how important you are to me," I said.

"Dad," he said, "you're doing fine. Are you going through one of those 'I'm being a bad father to Joey' phases again?"

"Maybe a small bout," I said, "but I really have had something big on my mind this past week. And I would like to bring you in on it."

"Shoot," he said, encouraging me onward.

I rallied my guts together and spat it out.

"Son," I said, "I'm planning to retire from the show when my contract expires in September."

"Retire?" Joey responded with incredulity. "Dad, you have the number one show in the nation right now!"

"I didn't know you followed the Nielsen Ratings."

"I don't," he grimaced. "Everyone I talk to reminds me of the fact."

"Well, nonetheless, I'm hanging up the hiking boots," I said.

"And doing what?" he asked.

"That's what I wanted to talk to you about."

Joey set down his fork and leaned in.

"I am going to make family my job," I said.

"Um," he chuckled, "you do know that I'm kind of the only one that falls into that category. Unless, of course, you are thinking of Grandma Margaret and Aunt Carol out in Boston."

"I'm interested in investing my life into you," I said. "What do you think?"

"Um, great," he said. "It sounds like quite the career demotion, and I'm not quite sure what it would mean to have my dad around all the time — but I guess I'm game."

"You know how you have told me that you always wished Mom and I had given you brothers and sisters?"

"Yeah," Joey replied while lifting an eyebrow curiously.

"Well, what would you think about adopting and sharing our life with some kids that could really use a helping hand?"

"What do you mean by that?" he asked.

"I'm glad you asked," I said with a wink. "I had a conversation with a social worker in Colorado yesterday."

"Why Colorado?" he asked.

"I'm considering getting out of L. A.," I said. "But I'm getting ahead of myself."

"You would leave SoCal?" he asked, his eyes wide open.

"Happily," I said. "But let me get back to the social worker in Colorado."

"Okay, sorry. Keep going," he said.

"She told me that she has three children in foster care, a boy and two girls, that desperately need a home — they need a father."

"And you are …" he muttered.

" — thinking that I might want to become that in their lives," I said, finishing his sentence.

"Are you serious?" he replied.

"I am," I said. "But only if you would be open to it."

Joey just sat there, bewildered. Part of him scared, part of him enthralled with the thought of having siblings.

"How old are they?"

"The boy is seventeen," I replied. "The girls are both sixteen."

"Whoa!" he muttered to himself. "A brother and two sisters?" Then he snapped his fingers and added, "Just like that."

"What do you think?" I asked.

"I think it's the craziest and coolest thing I may have ever heard in my life," he responded.

After dessert, I added a bit more detail about the three kids.

"These three kids have had a really rough go of it, Joey," I said. "I think the two of us could really make a difference in their lives."

I slid a note across the table and said, "Could you prayerfully ponder what is written on this paper?"

Here's what the note said:

> Joey,
> I discovered something else in my real estate research that I think you will find fabulously

flabbergasting. And it involves these three foster kids that we discussed tonight.

I realized that the most valuable real estate in the world is also THEM!

Worth the shed blood of Jesus Christ,
Worth His Almighty Life given up,
Worth God coming to Earth to save,
Worth God Himself suffering and dying,
Of inestimable, unfathomable worth.
Long and short, they are heavenly royalty.
I want to do this with you, Son!
Dad

Chapter Eight

Tears for Preciosa

February 2, 1979 changed me forever. Picking up Preciosa in my arms along the river bank was a moment I have relived and replayed over and over again in my mind these past five years.

I wanted to somehow try and share this experience with Joey. If possible, I wanted him to experience at least a small taste of it.

So, in April of this year, we hopped a Varig airlines flight to Brasília. Over the years, I had kept track of Preciosa's whereabouts, but I hadn't seen her since that magical day in the Amazon basin.

Five years earlier I had brought her to a Protestant church in Araras and entrusted her feeble little life to the pastor there. His name was Miguel Santos.

I said to him at the time, "This little treasure doesn't belong to the *Yacuruna*. She belongs to Jesus Christ."

He nodded in agreement, took her frail form in his arms, and sweetly and softly said into her ear, "You are Preciosa. That's your name, isn't it?"

From that moment, Miguel never let go of little

Preciosa. He became her father that day. Maria, his wife, became her mother. And little Preciosa became a Santos.

Miguel and Maria's ability to instantly adapt to the arrival of Preciosa in their lives was shocking to me.

In fact, the Santos' supernatural readiness to respond to an inconvenience — *any inconvenience, at any time* — has deeply convicted me, inspired me, and changed me.

Joey and I made the journey together to Araras. As we trekked through the thick jungle terrain, I retold to Joey the story of my Amazon awakening five years earlier. As we got closer and closer to the tiny Santos hut, I felt a growing anticipation. It was almost as if every step towards Preciosa was a step closer to the heart of God.

When we finally arrived at the bedraggled hut, I felt like tears were ready to literally explode from my eyes and weeping was ready to erupt from the depths of my soul.

And guess who answered the door?

Preciosa.

So beautiful. So precious. So perfect.

According to Joey, I "utterly embarrassed him" upon our arrival. Because, before I was even able to introduce him to Miguel and Maria, I picked up Preciosa in my arms, squeezed her tiny frame close, and cried for ten minutes straight.

Chapter Nine

Over the Hearth

Instead of returning from Brasília to Los Angeles, Joey and I flew directly to Colorado the following week in order to begin our search for a new home. God seemed to take us by the hand and lead us to the perfect spot, because we found something amazing. It was a cabin nestled in the pines at the foot of Dragon Mountain.

My episode, *Escaping Dragon Mountain* (originally aired in 1978), had been my most enduring and famous *Salt Worthy Adventures* installment over the years. To move my family to the foot of such a memorable location felt serendipitous — providential — extraordinary.

Standing in the living room next to my son, I looked up at the massive rock hearth and said, "I want to make an art piece to go right there!"

Sarah, our realtor, responded by saying, "Well, if you're interested, there's a well-known artist just about twenty minutes from here."

"I'm very interested," I said.

The artist's name was Dan Messer and he happened to be a woodcarver and pyrographer.

I sat down with Dan and explained precisely what I wanted. Dan simply nodded and said, "Let's do it."

Dan found a huge piece of live edge Maple burl that was ideal for the project.

At the very top of the piece he carved the words *The Doctrine of Exquisite Preciousness.*

And then underneath that grand title he pyrographed the following:

> *That which is unlovely — is loved*
> *That which is unholy — is pursued*
> *That which is unrighteous — is suffered for*
> *That which is unworthy — is died for*
> *That which is weak — is rescued*
> *And that which the world considers nothing —*
> *is exquisitely precious.*

When Dan finished, Joey and I hung this masterpiece above the mantel on the big rock hearth.

I'm in that very same mountain cabin right now as I write this. I'm sipping on a mug full of hot black coffee as I sit in my favorite brown leather chair. I turn my head slightly to the left and I see Dragon Mountain out through the big glass window. I turn my head to the right and I see Dan's piece of art.

All is peaceful at present.

The world is about to find out that I'm done with my television show after a ten-year run. After a bit more paperwork, one more social worker visit, and a trip to a local courthouse, I'm going to legally become the father of three amazing kids.

Their names: Price, Hannah, and Callie.

Long and short, a new adventure is just about to begin in my life.

So, as Aunt Carol and my dear mother might predict, I have a wry smile on my face, a chuckle in my throat, a glint in my eye, and my right hand is balled up into a fist.

Similar to the time I went over that waterfall in Brazil, I see the drop coming — it's just up ahead. Indubitably, it will be the ride of my life.

www.ingramcontent.com/pod-product-compliance
Lightning Source LLC
Chambersburg PA
CBHW072055040426
42447CB00012BB/3134